Don't Get
Your Knickers
in a Twist!

Paul Cookson is daft as a brush, mad as a hatter, as nutty as a fruitcake and busy as a bee. He spends most of his time visiting schools, libraries and literature festivals all over the country. Sometimes he's even invited! He performs his poems all over the shop, up hill and down dale, in the back of beyond – often with David Harmer as *Spill the Beans*. Paul is married to Sally and they have two children – Sam and Daisy.

While not preoccupied with the disturbance caused by the West London Panda Posse, Jane Eccles finds time between her career as a secret agent and her passion for illustrating Martian joke books from another world, she also illustrates books for earthlings.

Don't Get
Your Knickers
in a Twist!

Poems chosen by Paul Cookson

Illustrated by Jane Eccles

MACMILLAN CHILDREN'S BOOKS

*Dedicated to Ian, Jo, Lydia, Eleanor
and Madeleine   P.C.*

For Theo – with love from Mummy   J.E.

First published 2002
by Macmillan Children's Books
an imprint of Macmillan Publishers Limited
20 New Wharf Road, London N1 9RR
Basingstoke and Oxford
www.panmacmillan.com
Associated companies throughout the world

ISBN 0 330 39769 9

5 7 9 8 6 4

A CIP catalogue record for this book
is available from the British Library.

Printed by Mackays of Chatham plc, Chatham, Kent.

'Borrowed Time' © John Foster 2000 first published in *Climb Aboard the Poetry Plane*
by Oxford University Press and 'I'm Really Trying' © John Foster 2001 first published
in *Word Wizard* by Oxford University Press.
'Tongue in Cheek' © Judith Nicholls 1990 first published in *Dragonfire*
by Faber and Faber. Reprinted by permission of the author.
'Scatterbrain' by Gareth Owen first published in *Collected Poems* by
Macmillan Children's Books.

Contents

Chalk and Cheese

as different as chalk and cheese they say

but there's plenty of things

that are a lot more different than these

a blade of grass

and a pair of glass dungarees

for instance.

John Hegley

Today, I Feel

Today, I feel as:

Pleased as PUNCH,
Fit as a FIDDLE,
Keen as a KNIFE,
Hot as a GRIDDLE,

Bold as BRASS,
Bouncy as a BALL,
Keen as MUSTARD,
High as a WALL,

Bright as a BUTTON,
Light as a FEATHER,
Fresh as a DAISY,
Fragrant as HEATHER,

Chirpy as a CRICKET,
Sound as a BELL,
Sharp as a NEEDLE,
Deep as a WELL,
High as a KITE,
Strong as a BULL,
Bubbly as BATH WATER,
Warm as WOOL,
Clean as a new PIN,
Shiny as MONEY,
Quick as LIGHTNING,
Sweet as HONEY,

Cool as a CUCUMBER,
Fast as a HARE,
Right as RAIN,
Brave as a BEAR,
Lively as a MONKEY,
Busy as a BEE,
Good as GOLD,
Free as the SEA.

I'M SO HAPPY – I'M JUST LOST FOR WORDS.

Gervase Phinn

Ten Slightly Unfamiliar Sayings

There's no smoke without . . . well, a lot
of bits of wispy stuff floating around in
the air and smelling as if something's
been burned.

Every cloud has . . . an aeroplane in it.

Early to bed and early to rise . . . means
you miss all the late films on TV.

All work and no play . . . makes Jack a
completely unbelievable schoolboy.

A stitch in time saves . . . you from
  having to finish that cross-country race.
A friend in need . . . is probably someone
  you should avoid like the plague.
Too many cooks . . . means that you must
  have wandered into a training centre
  for TV chefs, or something.

Money is the root of all evil . . .
  but that's OK so long as I've
  got plenty.
The family that plays together . . .
  usually ends up having a huge
  row.
He who laughs last, laughs
  longest . . . unless you stuff an
  old sock in his mouth first.

Tony Bradman

Having My Ears Boxed

I am waiting in the corridor
To have my ears boxed.
I am nervous, for Mr O'Hanlon
Is a beast of his word.

For the last twenty minutes
I have let my imagination
Run away with itself.
But I am too scared to follow.

Will he use that Swiss Army knife
To slice through cleanly? Bite them off?
Tear carefully along perforated lines?
Tug sharply like loose Elastoplasts?

Acknowledging the crowd's roar
Will he hold my head aloft
As if it were the FA Cup
And pull the handles? Aagghhrr . . .

And then the box. Cardboard?
Old cigar-box possibly? Or a pair?
Separate coffins of polished pine.
L and R. 'Gone to a better place.'

Impatient now, I want to get it
Over with. Roll on four o'clock.
When, hands over where-my-ears-used-to-be
I run the gauntlet of jeering kids.

At six, Mother arrives home weary
After a hard day at the breadcrumb factory.
I give her the box. She opens it
And screams something. I say:

'Pardon?'

Roger McGough

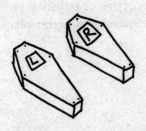

Keep Your Hair Ron!

Ron's wig cost a million pounds
I suppose that you could say
On Monday what he bought was
A high price toupee

When Tuesday's whirlwind blew it off
All it brought was sorrow
For what he didn't know on Monday was . . .
Hair today gone tomorrow.

Paul Cookson

A Drop in the Ocean

Sloshing around
in life's restless sea,
there's a drop in the ocean –
and that drop is me.

Riding the waves,
or washed up on the shore,
I'm a minuscule drop
amongst zillions more.

I'm a drop in the ocean
of life's restless sea –
but there'd be no ocean
without drops like me!

Jane Clarke

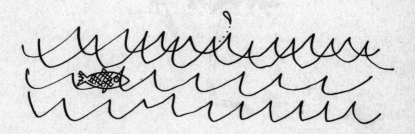

Last Legs

They say I'm on my last legs
And I can't go on much longer.
My first legs were much sprightlier
And sexier and stronger!
They sprang in time to Riverdance,
Leapt with Ballet Rambert –
Don't say I'm on my last legs!
Can't I have just *one* more pair?

Sue Cowling

Paws for Thought

My dog was staring at his feet,

Was it something he had caught?

Why no! My dog was thinking.

He was having paws for thought.

Roger Stevens

A Pearl of Wisdom

My world's an oyster,

I'm a pearl,

a highly polished, cultured girl

who once was shy

and didn't shine

but now I'm taken out to dine

on oysters.

Gina Douthwaite

Clichés

Every cloud has a silver lining;
Every rainbow, its pot of gold;
Every parting is such sweet sorrow;
Every story's a tale to be told;
Every joy is a joy for sharing;
Every bridge is just meant to be crossed;
Every day brings a new tomorrow;
Every win means that someone has lost;
Every song is a song worth singing;
Every dream has a chance to come true;
Every friend is a friend worth knowing –
So why am I lumbered with you?

Trevor Harvey

I'm Really Trying

My dad says my report is bad.

He says I must be lying

When I tell him that my teacher

Tells me I'm really trying.

John Foster

Driving Me Round the Bend!

I'd like to drive a tractor
   or maybe even a bus,
my mother says I drive her crazy
   by creating so much fuss.

I'd drive my brand new Honda
   do wheelies, skids and swerves.
I'd drive my father round the bend
   by getting on his nerves.

I'd like to drive at Silverstone
   and be part of the Grand Prix action,
my sister says I'm very good
   at driving people to distraction.

A driver's life is very hard
   you have to be tough and brave.
My family say that very soon
   I shall drive them to the grave!

John Rice

My Old Bear

has been in the wars,
has had the stuffing
knocked out of him
long since,
sits hunched
with shrivelled arms,
droops
limp ears,
glares
a single orange eye
like some tetchy colonel.

Given chance
he could tell
of escapades,
fighting the mumps,
soaking up tears,
getting through exams,
but seems content to rest
on the shelf,
kept in reserve
and not forgotten.

Barrie Wade

Some Sayings that Never Caught On

He's as daft as a pineapple!
Time is just like custard!
She swims like a cactus!

He's as daft as a cactus!
Time is just like a pineapple!
She swims like custard!

He's as daft as custard!
Time is just like a cactus!
She swims like a pineapple!

Ian McMillan

Scatterbrain

Before he goes to bed at night

Scatterbrained Uncle Pat

Gives the clock a saucer of milk

And winds up the tabby cat.

Gareth Owen

A Dog's Day

Every dog

Will have his day.

On my dog's day

He ran away.

Roger Stevens

Let Sleeping Dogs Lie

Hot dogs are toothless, yet prone to bite

And sharp enough to cut the mustard.

They never bark, but if you whisper

'Sausages' – a hissing sound is heard!

Bedded on onions, they satisfy;

Wrapped in rolls, let sleeping hot dogs lie.

Debjani Chatterjee

Lost Voice

Our teacher lost her voice
today . . .
        We don't know where it's gone,
we've searched all round the classroom
and all round the hall.

We've searched inside the cupboard,
we've looked behind the wall
and even in the toilets . . .
        It can't be found at all!

My mother says it's dreadful
my mother says it's sad . . .
        Miss Johnson only
        whispers
        But we are rather glad.

Peter Dixon

Borrowed Time

Great-Gran is ninety-six.
'I'm living on borrowed time,'
she said.

'Who did you borrow it from?'
asked my little sister.

'Never you mind,' said Gran.

'I hope you said thank you,'
said my sister.

Great-Gran laughed.
'I do,' she said.
'Every single day.'

John Foster

In for the High Jump

I'm not in the hurdles
I'm not in the sprints
I'm not in the skipping
   the throws
   or anything.
I'm not in the relay
Sports Day's what I dread
   but I know I'm for
   the high jump . . .
. . . for something that I said!

Peter Dixon

It Goes without Saying

Put your best foot forward
And hold your head up high
For to make a mint of money
Is not just pie in the sky.

I know the grass is greener
On the other side of the fence,
But the pounds will look after themselves
If you look after the pence . . .

So take notice of this saying;
Start saving for a rainy day;
Then the clouds will have a silver lining
And you'll be laughing all the way.

Alan Priestly

Burying the Hatchet

My friend is on the warpath

because I lost his tomahawk.

I only buried it in the garden for a joke

but when I couldn't find it

he hit me with his pipe of peace.

I don't think this game is working out.

Philip Waddell

Lettuce Pray

I'm standing here outside the headmaster's office
And it's all because of
that stupid word lettuce
AND IT'S THE WORST PLACE TO STAND IN THE
   WHOLE WORLD!
And it's hard to be fearless and
tearless when you're feeling
helpless and the whole
world feels airless
and it's all because of
that stupid word lettuce!
I'm sure Jesus liked a joke or two

(specially when He was my age),
don't you? And I'm sure He
wouldn't have been angry with me
or made me stand outside
His office all day
just because I said
lettuce pray.
I think I'll tell the Head
I didn't say
lettuce pray –
I'll say I said
lettuce pray
(after all they may).
If there was any justice in this school
the Head would just
lettuce go home.

Brian Patten

You Can't Teach an
Old Dog New Tricks

A pity because the ones they can do
   Are absolutely no use to you.
Amazing that when told, they 'stay'.
   But do they remember your mum's birthday?
Terrific at fetching sticks.
   Hopeless at writing limericks.
The best at chasing cats up trees.
   No good at patching dungarees?
Great at laying down to die.
   Useless at choosing a suitable tie.

– this one?

Brilliant at sitting up to beg.
　But a failure at making bacon and egg.
Perfect at offering you a paw.
　Not a clue about scrubbing the floor.
Wonderful at licking your face.
　No idea about packing a case.

If you're thinking of training your canine pet, it
Will be the best if you just forget it.

John Coldwell

Now Eat Your Hat

My Dad said,
if I made my bed
PROPERLY, he'd eat his hat.
So I did. When I said, Dad, I
made my bed PROPERLY! Now eat your hat –

he   off!
        bit   head
             my

Liz Brownlee

As Thick as Thieves

They only made a small mistake,

just couldn't get it right:

instead of stockings on their heads,

both wore *one* pair of tights.

Mike Johnson

Curtain-raiser

Break your duck
get off the mark
get set, get ready
to make a start

burst forth, switch on
step into that breach
set the ball rolling
it's your maiden speech

break the ice, take the plunge
clock your card and kick off
you're at concert pitch
and you're all teed-up

it's zero hour
D-day too
so get over the top
make your debut.

Stephen Clarke

Although

Although
I had

butterflies
in my
stomach

and ants
in my pants

and a bee
in my
bonnet

and a flea
in my
ear –

I had
a whale
of a time.

Tony Langham

Six of Mother Wise's
Seriously Silly Sayings

A stolen rose smells of fish.

Bedtime was invented by adults the moment they forgot they
were ever children.

The truth fluctuates according to the damage done.

Adults need more sleep than children because they are never quite as awake.

Toys are made by adults and sold in shops owned by adults but children still get the blame when they are too expensive.

The difference between a lie and a fib is that a fib might get you out of trouble, but a lie will always get someone else into trouble.

Brian Patten

Writer's Block

writer's block
writer's block
writer's block
writer's block

I've got

Coral Rumble

My Dad's Amazing!

My dad's **amazing** for he can:

make mountains out of molehills,
teach Granny to suck eggs,
make Mum's blood boil
and then drive her up the wall.

My dad's **amazing** for he also:

walks around with his head in the clouds,
has my sister eating out of his hand,
says he's got eyes in the back of his head
and can read me like a book.

But,
the most **amazing** thing of all is:

when he's caught someone red-handed,
first he jumps down their throat
and then he bites their head off!

Ian Souter

...I can see what you're up to!

Visitor

This summer

A distant cousin came to stay

But I didn't see him

He always was too far away

Roger Stevens

Don't Get Your Knickers in a Twist!

We never knew that Mum could be a great contortionist
Until the underwear she wore decided to resist
She aimed straight for the legholes but somehow they
   missed . . .
In a spot the day she got her knickers in a twist.

They restricted and constricted her like an iron fist
Held hostage by the tightening elastic terrorist
One leg round her head and the other round her wrist . . .
A human knot the day she got her knickers in a twist.

She struggled, strained and wrestled but they would not desist
The wrangling and the strangling continued to persist
Walking like an alien exhibitionist
A hop, a squat, a trot, she's got her knickers in a twist.

Trussed up like a chicken, peering through her legs she hissed,
'Help me quick! What I need's a physiotherapist.'
Dad's reply was casual and utterly dismissed . . .
When he said, 'Do not fret
There's no need to panic yet
Play it cool, just don't get your knickers in a twist.'

Paul Cookson

Sam Spade Sums Up

All she'd seen were his eyes
lying on the doormat,
wide open and looking round.
He must have dropped them
when he heard her coming.
Hanging from the chandelier
was the skin out of which
he had obviously jumped.

Unable to give further information,
her heart being in her mouth
and good manners forbade
talking with her mouth full,
she sank into a chair.
Out of her depth she left us
to fathom the mystery.

We knew he had been
up to his neck in it;
his collar witnessed that.
But his shoes showed
a clean pair of heels.
The only skin left to him
was on his teeth
and that wouldn't save him.

As we caught up with him
everything fell into place.
A body search revealed
guilt written all over him.
Under fierce grilling
he went to pieces.
His jaw dropped
and spoke for itself.

John C. Desmond

Early to Bed Early to Rise

The early bird catches the worm;
He is early to bed and to rise.
   For him worms equal wealth
   And in matters of health
Such habits as these are wise.
   But the worm, poor dull beast,
   (Who takes part in this feast)
Does not know the sayings of old.
   With nocturnal wandering
   His life he is squandering,
(What a pity he never was told).
   If only they'd said
   About early to bed,
Given warning re going to bed late,
   He'd have been tucked away
   At the breaking of day
And not on some bird's breakfast plate.

Catherine Benson

Them

'If you ask me,' she said,
'They're two sandwiches short of a picnic
Cos their heads aren't screwed on right
So they act the goat,
Monkey around,
Get up to no good
And, when all's said and done,
Behave like a set of complete idioms.'

Nick Toczek

Lucky for Me

This morning
the bus driver gave me the wrong change
so I told him and he said
I'd got my head screwed on right
and I thought of all those unhappy people
who haven't.

They must have really wonky heads
like badly fitting light bulbs
you call their name
and if they look round too fast
their heads will spin
round and round
until their bonces
bounce down the street.

When the wind is blowing hard
they have to stay indoors
to stop their head blowing away
like a big balloon
they mustn't panic
or they will lose their heads
if they play football and nod in a goal
their bobbing beezer follows the ball
if they disagree with you too strongly
their boko shakes loose at the neck
when they go to sleep at night
they twiddle off their heads
put them in a bowl beside the bed.

It must be really difficult
no wonder so many people wear
those baseball caps
they ram them down to keep
their heads from dropping off.

But I'm OK
I've pulled and tugged
shoved and shaken
it hasn't moved
I've got my head screwed on right
so there.

David Harmer

Running

Above the tap it said
'Run a long time
to get hot water.'

So I ran round the room for a really long time
but I didn't get any hot water.

Michael Rosen

A Poem Written on Behalf of Parrots against the Continual Use of 'As sick as a Parrot' as a Simile Expressing Extreme Disappointment

Why always say 'as sick as a parrot'
Why not 'as sick as a moose'?
Why not 'as sick as a poodle'?
Or 'as sick as a barnacle goose'?

Why not 'as sick as a giant panda'?
As a racoon or a polar bear?
Why load it all on to parrots?
It really isn't fair!

So please give parrots a break now.
'Sick as a parrot' – no way Jose!
Choose another creature to feature
Instead of this tired, old cliché!

Tony Langham

The Grass is Always Greener on the Other Side

Mr Smith – he loved his lawn
He watered it at crack of dawn.
But Mr Harris, who lived next door,
Did no more
Than sleep on his deckchair and snore.

Mr Smith – dragged a rake
a mower and roller for his lawn's sake
But Mr Harris, who lived next door,
Did no more
Than sleep on his deckchair and snore.

Mr Smith – spread fertilizer
sprayed on with an atomizer
But Mr Harris, who lived next door,
Did no more
Than sleep on his deckchair and snore.

Mr Smith peered over his wall
At Mr Harris doing nothing at all
'It's not fair,' he jealously cried
'That your lawn is green
While my lawn has died.'
Mr Harris turned in his sleep to moan,
'Lawns grow best when left alone.'

John Coldwell

Under the Weather

I hate being under the weather.
It's cold down here.
And damp.

I'd rather be over the moon
or head in the clouds.
Flying high.
Staring at stars.

Everything's getting on top of me.
I hate being under the weather.

Bernard Young

Ignorance

They say that ignorance is bliss,

And Tom is living proof of this:

He's ignorant of many things,

And yet how merrily he sings,

Whilst others, wiser far than he,

Are gloomy to the *nth* degree.

Colin West

The Reader of this Poem

The reader of this poem
Is as cracked as a cup
As daft as treacle toffee
As mucky as a pup

As troublesome as bubblegum
As brash as a brush
As bouncy as a double-tum
As quiet as a sshhh . . .

As sneaky as a witch's spell
As tappy-toe as jazz
As empty as a wishing-well
As echoey as as as as as as . . . as . . . as . . .

As bossy as a whistle
As prickly as a pair
Of boots made out of thistles
And elephant hair

As vain as trainers
As boring as a draw
As smelly as a drain is
Outside the kitchen door

As hungry as a wave
That feeds upon the coast
As gaping as the grave
As GOTCHA! as a ghost

As fruitless as a cake of soap
As creeping-up as smoke
The reader of this poem, I hope,
Knows how to take a joke!

Roger McGough

Quite the Opposite

There are chores to be done and maybe
You're sometimes inclined to shirk,
And your mum may trot out that old proverb:
'Come on. *Many Hands Make Light Work.*'

There's a proverb by way of reply,
Though you may risk your mother's wrath.
I suggest that you smile as your answer:
'Yes, but *Too Many Cooks Spoil the Broth.*'

Eric Finney

Robinson Crusoe's Wise Sayings

You can never have too many turtle's eggs.
I'm the most interesting person in this room.
A beard is as long as I want it to be.

The swimmer on his own doesn't need trunks.
A tree is a good clock.
If you talk to a stone long enough you'll fall asleep.

I know it's Christmas because I cry.
Waving at ships is useless.
Footprints make me happy, unless they're my own.

Ian McMillan

Tongue in Cheek

My heart's in my mouth,
my brain has been washed –
my tongue's in my cheek.

I've a chip on my shoulder,
I've brought up a child –
I'm feeling quite weak.

I've paid through the nose,
made a pig of myself –
you should take a peek.

I'm pulling a face,
here's a piece of my mind –
I really can't speak.

My eyes are the size
of three stomachs or more –
my tongue's in my cheek.

Judith Nicholls

It's Not My Cup of Tea

It's not my cup of tea,
It's just not the thing for me.
Not my burger, not my chips,
Not my spicy salsa dips,
Not my sweet and sour chicken,
It just isn't finger-lickin'.
Not my cheeseburger and fries,
Not my steak and kidney pies,
Not my sausages and fritter,
Not my pizza margarita,
Not my cola, not my juice,
Not my sticky chocolate mousse,
Not my rum-and-raisin ice,
It just isn't very nice.
Really not the thing for me.
No! It's not my cup of tea!

Paul Bright

You'll Look Like One

'If you eat any more lollies
you'll start to look like one,'
Mum says.

'Well, what about you
and your cups of tea,
the same goes for you
as it does for me!'

I picture my mum
as a huge mug of tea
and me as a three-flavoured
drink on a stick.

'What's more,' she says,
'don't make that face.
The wind will change
and leave you stuck!'

Knowing my luck
that's probably true!

I fix my face in
a fresh grimace,
the mug of tea wobbles
then smiles:

'Be off with you,'
she says,
and like a lolly
I melt away!

Brian Moses

Watching Nails Go Rusty

We seemed to do a lot of it
when I was a child.
At least that's what Dad said it was like
when it took me ages to get a job done
or longer than usual to get ready for church.

The Test Match on a slow day,
an uneventful England International football match
or waiting for the rain to stop on holiday
would also fit this category.

Personally speaking,
visiting aged female relatives
in old-fashioned houses
with tea in bone-china cups and saucers
where you had to sit still and not play
or talk until you were spoken to,
or overlong sermons on hot summer days
also qualified,
although I never said so.

Yes, we used to do a lot of it then,
watching nails go rusty.
That, and paint drying.
Sometimes, we'd do it till the cows came home.

Paul Cookson

Drop-dead Gorgeous

I'm drop-dead gorgeous,
can't you see?
Drop-dead gorgeous,
yes, that's me.
No film producers
have got me yet.
I am playing hard to get.
Drop-dead gorgeous!
Models cry
and gnash their teeth
As I walk by.
Drop-dead gorgeous . . .
'Wake up!' Mum screams.
Drop-dead gorgeous?
In my dreams.

Marian Swinger

Truth

Sticks and stones may break my bones,
but words can also hurt me.
Stones and sticks break only skin,
while words are ghosts that haunt me.

Slant and curved the word-swords fall
to pierce and stick inside me.
Bats and bricks may ache through bones,
but words can mortify me.

Pain from words has left its scar
on mind and heart that's tender.
Cuts and bruises now have healed;
it's words that I remember.

Barrie Wade

The Writer of this Poem

The writer of this poem
Is taller than a tree
As keen as the North wind
As handsome as can be

As bold as a boxing-glove
As sharp as a nib
As strong as scaffolding
As tricky as a fib

As smooth as a lolly-ice
As quick as a lick
As clean as a chemist-shop
As clever as a ✓

The writer of this poem
Never ceases to amaze
He's one in a million billion
(or so the poem says!)

Roger McGough

Having a Brainstorm

I can always tell
When my Dad
Is having
A brainstorm

Lightning usually
Shoots out of his ears
And when he rolls

His eyes, you can hear
The rumble of
Distant thunder.

Tony Langham

His Days Were Numbered!

The champion entered the ring
as the undisputed No 1.
In new silk shorts
and matching dressing gown
he was dressed to the nines
but also in A1 condition!
The challenger –
who had stood in at the 11th hour –
was supposed to be second rate
and was a thousand-to-one outsider!

At the bell they quickly
squared up to each other
but as expected by everyone
the champion was first off the mark.
No second thoughts, no quarter given,
A quick one, two combination
and the challenger was hit for six!

But on this particular night
the champion only had half a mind
on the task at hand
until as the fight progressed
his sixth sense began to warn him
that if he wasn't careful
his number would soon be up!

And so it was to prove,
as the determined challenger
now put two and two together,
and using double-quick reflexes,
as well as ten out of ten for technique
he soon had the champion at sixes and sevens
and before he had a second chance
the fight became too one-sided
and the champion's reign
was finally at an end.

Unfortunately, it would seem that winning
had become second nature to him
or, perhaps it had been one fight too many,
but as far as the challenger was concerned
he really couldn't care less
for he was now in seventh heaven.

And so the champion had
finally been beaten to the punch!
He was back to square one
for the champion was now once again –
the challenger!

Ian Souter

Waking the Dead

'You're making enough noise
to wake the dead!'
shrieked their mum.
Up in the attic
a ghost yawned and stretched
and groped for its specs.
'Vanished into thin air!
I might as well be looking for
a needle in a haystack,'
it grouched.
'It's like Aladdin's cave
with all the junk
they've got up here.'
When the kids were in bed
the ghost materialized
beside their bunk beds.
'I've a bone to pick with you,'
it said, waving one
(from its leg actually).
'I am not exactly over the moon
with that horrible row you've been making.
In fact, you've really got my goat.'
'You got out of bed
on the wrong side didn't you?'
chorused the kids.
'Cheeky brats,' grumbled the ghost,
'just riding roughshod over my feelings.
We'll see how you like it.'
Then it wailed like a banshee.

It kept it up all night.
The kids didn't get a wink of sleep.
It vanished at the crack of dawn
never to return
and found a lonely churchyard
with a nice detached tomb
with no chain.
It moved in straightaway.
It was a real home from home.

Marian Swinger

Over the Moon!

I'm over the moon!
Never had better reason to smile.
We were crazy about one another, though,
Just for a while.
When I look at its face now
I wonder what I used to see.
No, I'm over the moon –
But I'm not sure the moon's over me!

Sue Cowling

Give a Dog a Bad Name

I was walking in the park

When I heard a dog bark

I hoped that it would be worse than his bite

But something I saw, made me take flight.

I knew for certain that dog was not tame

As the tag round his neck said, 'Bad Name'.

John Coldwell

Going Nowhere Fast

Road Works
Delays Expected Until September

On the motorway, in the passenger seat,
I look at my watch . . .
Ten past three on the twenty-sixth.
Of March.
And we could be here till September?
That's five, no six months!
We haven't brought any sandwiches.
No telly.
No toilet.
No nothing.

Just cars. And cars.
And lorries. And caravans. And more cars.
As the traffic grinds to a juddering halt
So does my heart as time stands still
and we start going nowhere . . .
fast.

Paul Cookson

An Odd Kettle of Fish

The detectives said that
The books had been cooked.
(They tasted good.)

My teacher said we could
have a free hand.
(I added it to my collection.)

Some people bottle up
their feelings.
(I keep mine in a jar.)

My mother said –
'Hold your tongue!'
(It was too slippery.)

When my sister laughs
she drives me round the bend.
(I catch the bus back.)

Dad told me
to keep a stiff upper lip.
(It's in a box by my bed.)

My uncle is a terrible
name-dropper.
(I help my aunt to sweep them up.)

In the school races
I licked everyone in the class.
(It made my tongue sore.)

Pie Corbett

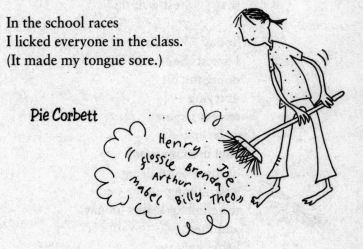

Rest Assured?

Yesterday my mother
was speaking
on the phone to somebody.

I don't know
who it was,
possibly God
or someone in government
because she said,
'It is very important
in all this
that you rest a shore.'

Today
I am at the beach
doing my bit
in trying
to rest a shore.

Saying to the sand,
'it must be so tiring
entertaining
the clinking waves all day
and then
being kept up
at night
by the bright, partying moon.'

So I didn't
bring my frisbee
or bucket and spade.
I heard what my mother said,
she sounded quite serious,
because it's very important
to rest a shore.

Stewart Henderson

Ha Ha! 100 Hundred Poems to Make You Laugh

Chosen by Paul Cookson

By the very best poets around, from
Valerie Bloom to Charles Causley to Brian Patten

Dragon Love Poem

*when you smile
the room lights up*

*and I have to call
the fire brigade.*

Roger Stevens

The Evil Doctor Mucus Spleen
and Other Superbad Villains

Poems chosen by Paul Cookson

Meet the criminal masterminds who are plotting to take over
the world in this dastardly collection of villainous poetry.

The Evil Doctor Mucus Spleen

Whose operations and routines
take science to the dark extremes?
Who's part-alien, part-machine?

His cauldrons bubble, test-tubes fizz,
sockets hum and wires whizz.
I bet you know just who it is . . .
The Evil Evil Evil . . . Doctor Mucus Spleen!

He's mean! He's green! He'll make you scream!
The baddest villain ever seen!
Watch out for his laser-beam!
The Evil Evil Evil Evil Doctor Mucus Spleen!

Paul Cookson

SUPERHEROES

Fearless poems chosen by Paul Cookson

SITUATION VACANT
COULD YOU BE

our next trainee Superhero/heroine?

Immediate vacancy exists for this challenging post
With excitement and adventure guaranteed uppermost.
Your duty will be to save the planet Earth
From an evil and imminent alien invasion.
Starting salary by negotiation.
Expected age range from twenty through to forty.
Applicants should be fit and keen and sporty.
Ability to fly (without wings) even better.
          Apply now, by letter,
          With full details and C.V.
                    To:–
          Save the World plc.
          P.O. Box 303
          Gotham City
                    USA
(Closing date for applications is the 31st May)

Alan Priestley

A selected list of poetry books available from Macmillan

The prices shown below are correct at the time of going to press.
However, Macmillan Publishers reserve the right to show new retail prices
on covers which may differ from those previously advertised.

The Evil Doctor Mucus Spleen	0 330 39717 6
Poems chosen by Paul Cookson	£3.99
The Very Best of Paul Cookson	0 330 48014 6
Poems by Paul Cookson	£3.99
Who Rules the School?	0 330 35199 0
Poems chosen by Paul cookson	£3.50
Superheroes	0 330 48262 9
Fearless poems, chosen by Paul Cookson	£2.99
Tongue Twisters and Tonsil Twizzlers	0 330 34941 4
Poems chosen by Paul Cookson	£3.50
Let's Twist Again	0 330 37559 8
Poems chosen by Paul Cookson	£2.99
Ridiculous Relatives	0 330 37105 3
Poems chosen by Paul Cookson	£3.50

All Macmillan titles can be ordered at your local bookshop
or are available by post from:

Book Service by Post
PO Box 29, Douglas, Isle of Man IM99 1BQ

Credit cards accepted. For details:
Telephone: 01624 675137
Fax: 01624 670923

E-mail: bookshop@enterprise.net

Free postage and packing in the UK.
Overseas customers: add £1 per book (paperback)
and £3 per book (hardback)